My First Animal Library

River Otters

by Cari Meister

Bullfrog Books

Ideas for Parents and Teachers

Bullfrog Books let children practice reading informational text at the earliest reading levels. Repetition, familiar words, and photo labels support early readers.

Before Reading

- Discuss the cover photo. What does it tell them?

- Look at the picture glossary together. Read and discuss the words.

Read the Book

- "Walk" through the book and look at the photos. Let the child ask questions. Point out the photo labels.

- Read the book to the child, or have him or her read independently.

After Reading

- Prompt the child to think more. Ask: River otters live in North America. Have you ever spotted one?

Bullfrog Books are published by Jump!
5357 Penn Avenue South
Minneapolis, MN 55419
www.jumplibrary.com

Library of Congress Cataloging-in-Publication Data

Names: Meister, Cari, author.
Title: River otters / by Cari Meister.
Other titles: Bullfrog books. My first animal library.
Description: Minneapolis, MN : Jump!, Inc., [2018]
Series: My first animal library | Audience: Ages 5–8. | Audience: K to grade 3. | Includes index.
Identifiers: LCCN 2017042579 | 9781624967610 (ebook)
ISBN ISBN 9781624967603 (hardcover : alk. paper)
Subjects: LCSH: North American river otter—Juvenile literature. | Otters—Juvenile literature.
Classification: LCC QL737.C25 M3785 2018
DDC 599.769/2—dc23
LC record available at https://lccn.loc.gov/2017042579

Editor: Jenna Trnka
Book Designer: Leah Sanders

Photo Credits: Jerryway/Dreamstime, cover; ZSSD/Minden Pictures/SuperStock, 1; mojoeks/Shutterstock, 3; Rudmer Zwerver/Shutterstock, 4; davidhoffmann photography/Shutterstock, 5; MarcQuebec/iStock, 6–7; stephen rudolph/Shutterstock, 8, 23br; Kris Wiktor/Shutterstock, 8–9; Paul Christian Gordon/Alamy, 10–11, 23tr; Jillian Cooper/iStock, 12; Minden Pictures/SuperStock, 13, 18–19, 23tl; Polina Truver/Shutterstock, 14–15; Juniors BildarchivGmbH/Alamy, 16; milehightraveler/iStock, 17; Andrew Kandel/Alamy, 20–21, 23bl; MiozB/Shutterstock, 22; EML/Shutterstock, 24.

Printed in the United States of America at Corporate Graphics in North Mankato, Minnesota.

Table of Contents

Made to Swim

An otter slides down a hill.
Where is it going?

To the river!

The otter has
a long body.

It can twist.

It can turn.

It has webbed feet.
They paddle.

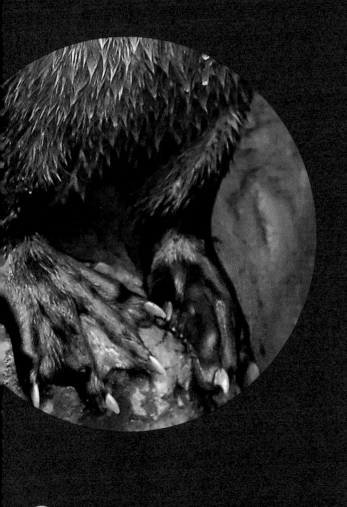

tail

It has a strong tail.

The otter uses
it to steer.

The otter grabs a fish.
The fish wiggles.

But the otter's teeth hang on.

The otter is
on its back.

Thick fur helps
it float.

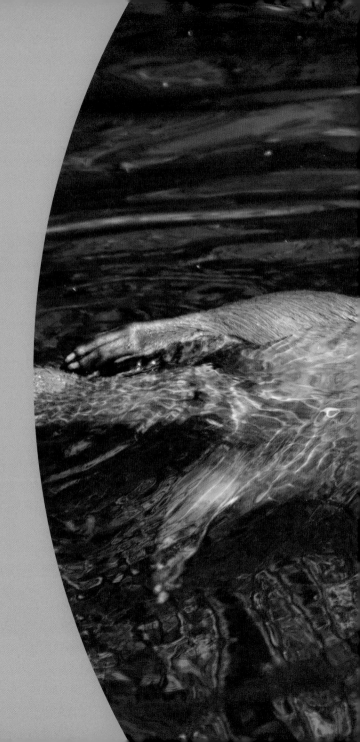

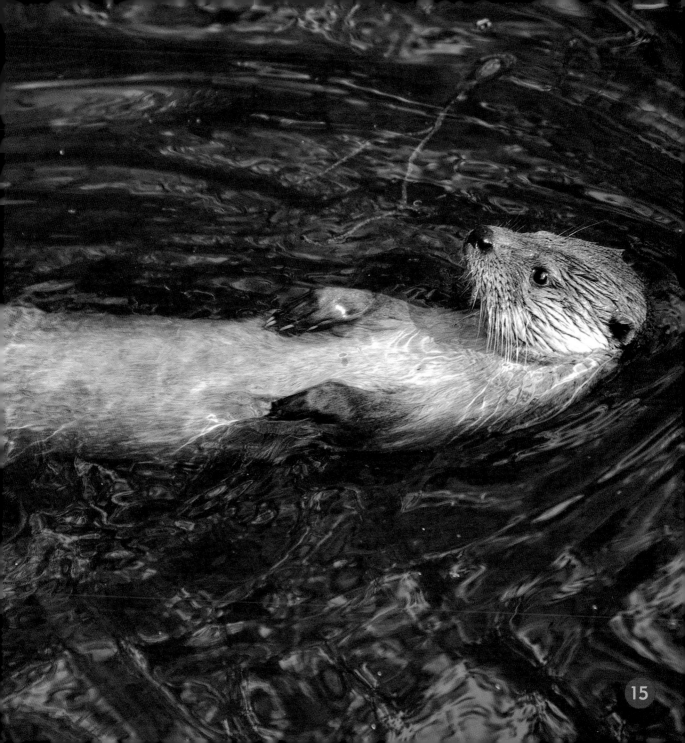

Otters love to have fun.
They chase their tails.

They play with each other.

tunnel

den

Otters live in dens.
They are by the water.
They use tunnels
to get in and out.

This otter catches a fish.

She teaches her pup.

This is how the pup learns.

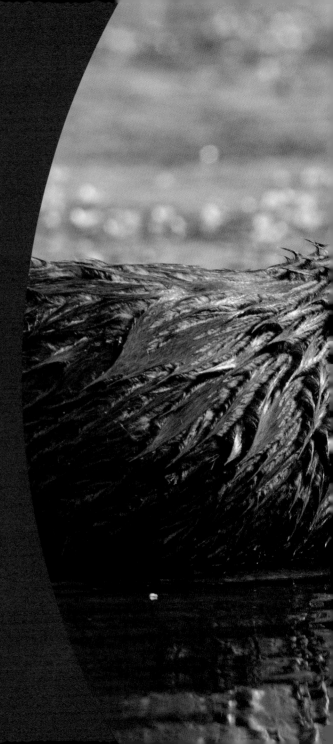

pup

Parts of a River Otter

fur
An otter's thick fur repels water and keeps the otter warm.

whiskers
An otter's whiskers sense movement to help find food.

body
An otter's body is long and flexible.

tail
An otter has a strong, long tail. It helps the otter swim faster and steer in the water.

feet
An otter has webbed feet that help it swim fast.

Picture Glossary

dens
Cave or holes otters live in.

steer
To guide or direct movement.

pup
A young otter.

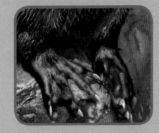
webbed
To have skin between the toes.

Index

To Learn More

Learning more is as easy as 1, 2, 3.

1) Go to www.factsurfer.com

2) Enter "riverotters" into the search box.

3) Click the "Surf" button to see a list of websites.

With factsurfer.com, finding more information is just a click away.